Let Sleeping Dogs Lie

Book 1 of the

Mr. Nibbles' Bites of Life

Series

By Mr. Nibbles and
Leslie Adebonojo

Spring Knoll Press

2018

This book is a work of fiction. The character in this story, Mr. Nibbles, does not represent any other dog. Any resemblance to any other dog living or dead is entirely coincidental.

Copyright © 2018 by Leslie Adebonojo

All rights reserved.

Published in the United States.

Spring Knoll Press

ISBN 9780997874648

For Geoff

You always encouraged me to do it, so, I did it with pictures.

Love, mom

For parents – discussions and observations you may want to have with your child.

Page

1 – What is an animal shelter? Why do animals live in a shelter? Why do you think the dog's name is Mr. Nibbles? (Hint: He likes to nibble on your toes and fingers, but never too hard).

3 – What type of exercise does a dog need to be happy? Do different dog breeds need more exercise? What is a dog breed?

9 – Why do some dogs eat grass? What do dogs eat?

10 – Look at the tree in the picture. Can you tell what season it is? What is a season?

11 – How many rocks did Mr. Nibbles climb up on?

12 – Look at the tree. Can you tell what season it is?

13 – What adventure would you like to have?

14 – Mr. Nibbles doesn't want to fall asleep. He wants to keep playing.

19 & 20 – Where is the rest of Mr. Nibbles? Does the blanket in the picture have stripes that remind you of another animal?

23 & 24 Is there a difference between the pictures on these two pages?

Contact your local animal shelter to find out more about adopting a pet.

Mr. Nibbles came from a local animal shelter to live with us.
He loves to run outside,
play ball,
and most of all sleep.

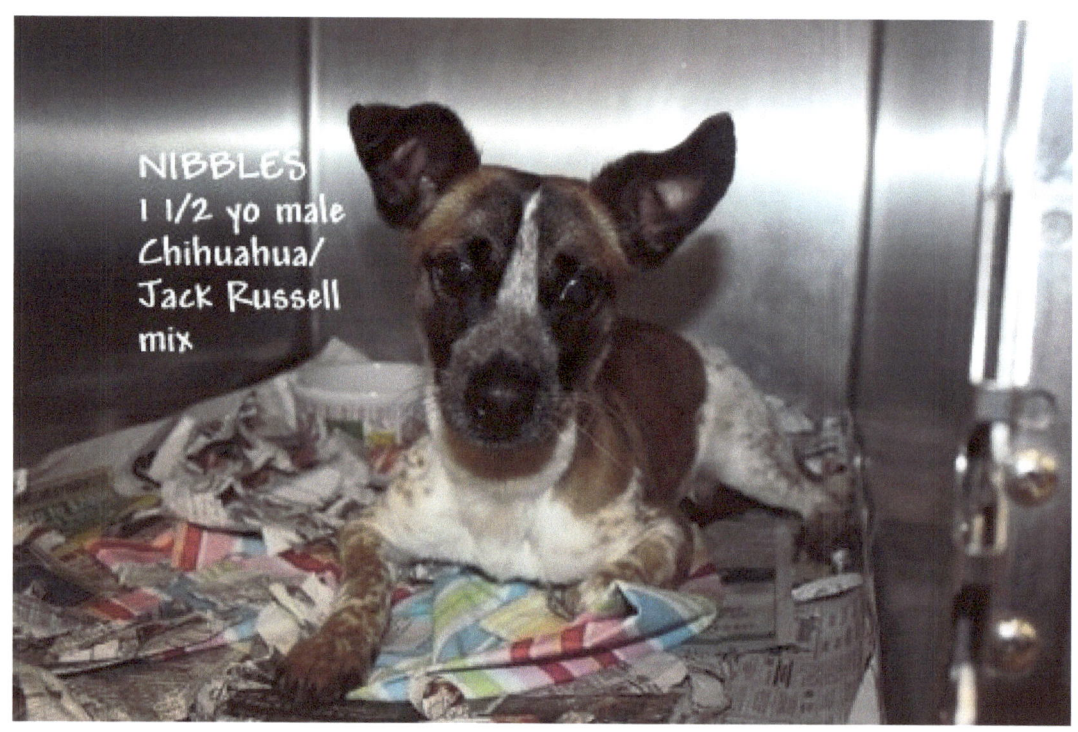

With lots of love and plenty of vegetables (he loves carrots and green beans), Mr. Nibbles grew strong and playful.

Play ball, please!

We go outside.

Looking for that yummy new grass.

Where is Mr. Nibbles?

Mr. Nibbles jumped on every rock he could find.

Where is Mr. Nibbles?

My next adventure is out there somewhere. I know it!

Oh, no, I'm getting

sleepy.

Mr. Nibbles is dreaming about a lion. Do you see the lion?

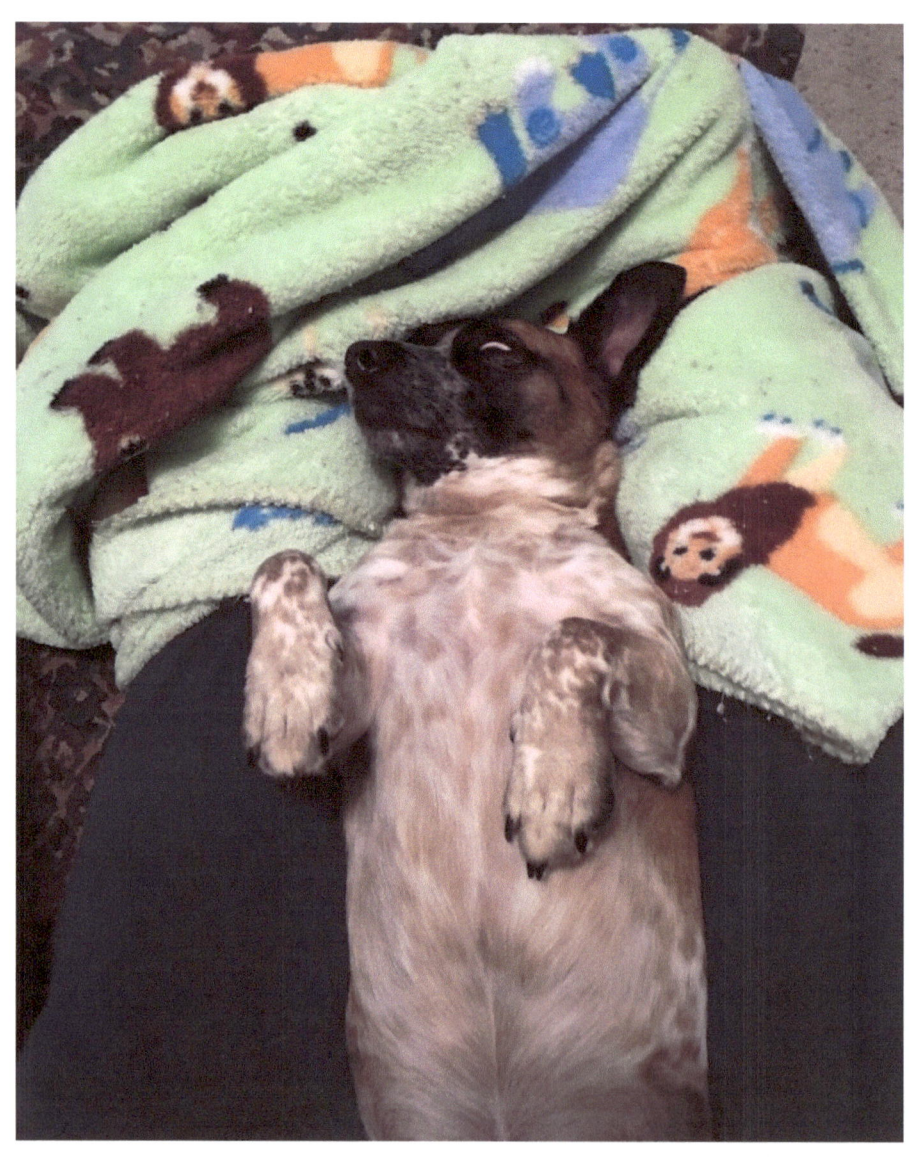

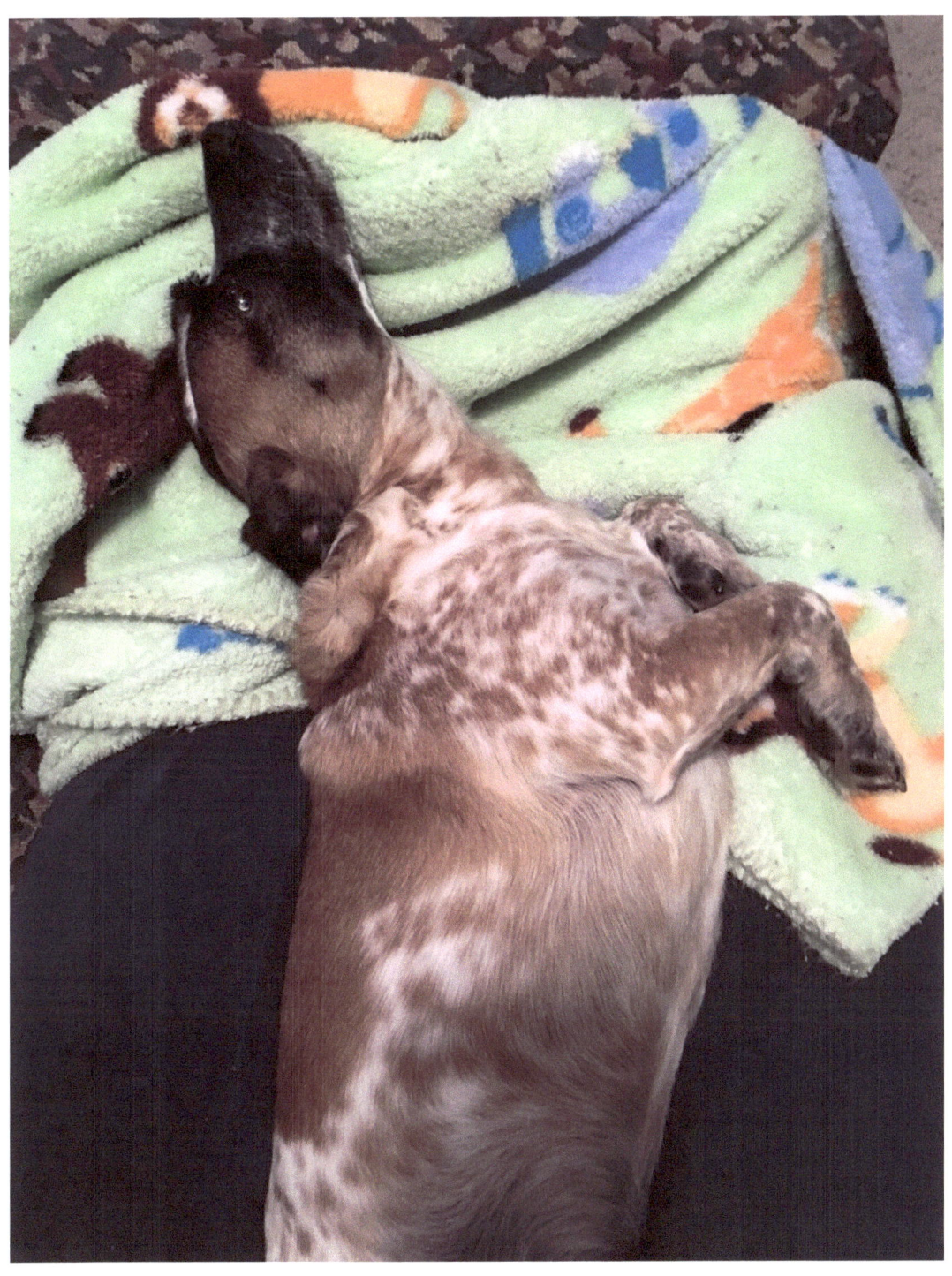

Are you taking my picture again?

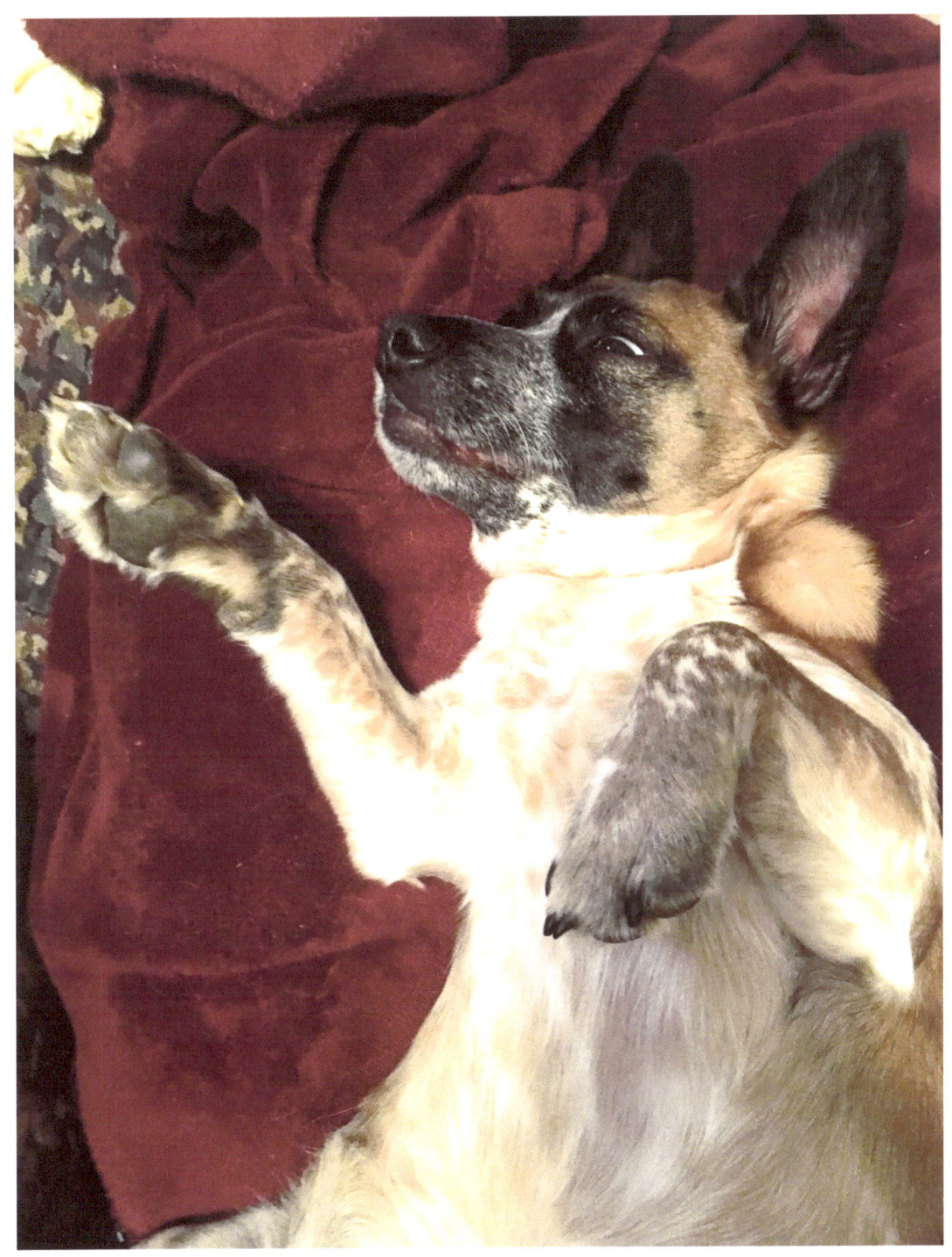

Time to play ball again, please!

Bye, Bye.

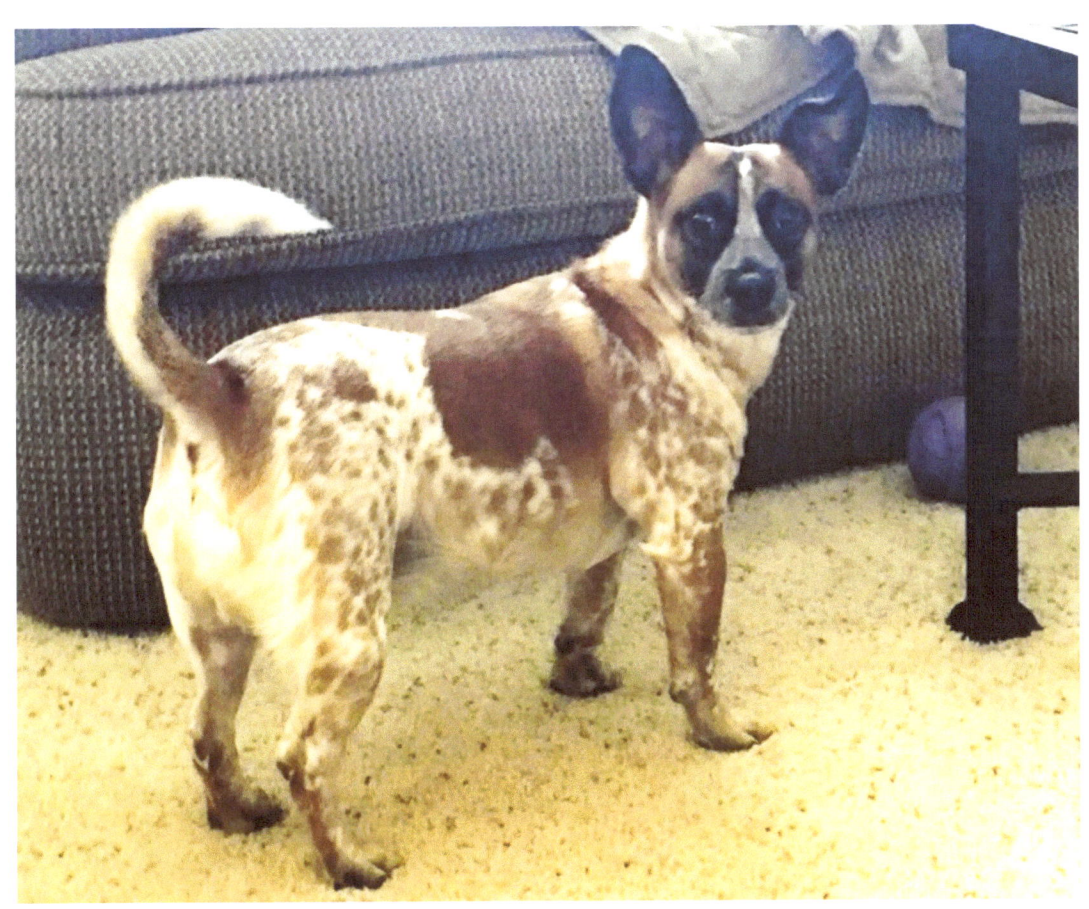

www.ingramcontent.com/pod-product-compliance
Lightning Source LLC
LaVergne TN
LVHW071029070426
835507LV00002B/84